THE VEGGIE BURGER COOKBOOK

50 DELICIOUS VEGGIE BURGER RECIPES THAT EVERYONE WILL LOVE

By
BookSumo Press
Copyright © by Saxonberg Associates
All rights reserved

Published by
BookSumo Press, a DBA of Saxonberg Associates
http://www.booksumo.com/

JOIN THE BOOKSUMO PRIVATE READER'S CLUB AND GET A MASSIVE COLLECTION OF 6 COOKBOOKS!

The first set of cookbook is for the lovers of easy cooking.

You will get the "Easy Specialty Cookbook Box Set" for FREE!

This box set includes the following cookbooks:

1. Easy Sushi Cookbook
2. Easy Dump Dinner Cookbook
3. Easy Beans Cookbook

AND for the ethnic and cultural food lovers you will also get the "Easy Cultural Cookbook Box Set" for FREE as well!

This box set includes the following cookbooks:

1. A Kitchen in Morocco
2. Easy Samosas & Pot Pie Recipes
3. The Biryani Bash

Join the group of private readers, and enjoy these cookbooks. This collection is only available for private readers and it's over 400 pages when printed! Plus you will receive fun updates, and musings about food and cooking.

6 Cookbooks. 400+ pages of recipes. Everything delicious and easy.

To get these 6 free books just stay to the end of this cookbook and follow the directions at the back!

ABOUT THE AUTHOR.

BookSumo Press is a publisher of unique, easy, and healthy cookbooks.

Our cookbooks span all topics and all subjects. If you want a deep dive into the possibilities of cooking with any type of ingredient. Then BookSumo Press is your go to place for robust yet simple and delicious cookbooks and recipes. Whether you are looking for great tasting pressure cooker recipes or authentic ethic and cultural food. BookSumo Press has a delicious and easy cookbook for you.

With simple ingredients, and even simpler step-by-step instructions BookSumo cookbooks get everyone in the kitchen chefing delicious meals.

BookSumo is an independent publisher of books operating in the beautiful Garden State (NJ) and our team of chefs and kitchen experts are here to teach, eat, and be merry!

INTRODUCTION

Welcome to *The Effortless Chef Series*! Thank you for taking the time to purchase this cookbook.

Come take a journey into the delights of easy cooking. The point of this cookbook and all BookSumo Press cookbooks is to exemplify the effortless nature of cooking simply.

In this book we focus on Veggie Burgers. You will find that even though the recipes are simple, the taste of the dishes are quite amazing.

So will you take an adventure in simple cooking? If the answer is yes please consult the table of contents to find the dishes you are most interested in.

Once you are ready, jump right in and start cooking.

— BookSumo Press

TABLE OF CONTENTS

About the Author.

Introduction

Table of Contents

Any Issues? Contact Us

Legal Notes

Common Abbreviations

Chapter 1: Easy Veggie Burger Recipes

    Summer Soy Burgers

    Provolone Caps Burgers

    Crunchy Cheddar Bean Burgers

    Thai Bell Bean Burgers

    Latin Chili Burgers

    White Oyster Burgers

    Red Parmesan Burgers

    Black Seafood Burgers

    Korean Barbecue Burgers

    Barbecue Cheddar Burgers

- Jack's Hickory Jalapeno Burgers
- Quaker Corn Burgers
- Latin Salsa Burgers
- Hot Chili Braggs Burgers
- Peanut Butter Burgers
- Braggs' Oat Burgers
- Chili Romano Burgers
- Curry Nuts Burgers
- White Steak Burgers
- Rolled Kidney Bean Burgers
- Tamari Burger Casserole
- Sea Lentils Burgers
- Beasty Garbanzo Burgers
- Balsamic Mayo Burgers
- Parmesan Kernels Burger
- Baby Cheddar Burger
- Nutty Teriyaki Burges
- Farmer's Market Burger
- Saucy Vegan Burger
- Chili Corn Burgers

Nuts Burger

Chipotle Cannellini Burgers

Red Pecans Burgers

Bell Artichoke Burgers

Hollywood Burgers

Chili Mexican Black Bean Burgers

Amaranth Millet Burgers

Juicy Beet Burgers

Sweet and Spicy Burger

Late October Tahini Burgers

Old Bay Burgers

Sesame Burgers

Cajun Burgers with Lemon Sauce

Oregon Inspired Burgers

Cereal Mayo Burgers

Asian Italian Burgers with Cajun Mayo

London Shiitake Worcestershire Burgers

Portobello Pepperjack Monterey Spicy Burgers

Eggplant Patties with Cheddar

Horseradish Mushroom Burger I

Zucchini Burgers

ANY ISSUES? CONTACT US

If you find that something important to you is missing from this book please contact us at info@booksumo.com.

We will take your concerns into consideration when the 2nd edition of this book is published. And we will keep you updated!

— BookSumo Press

LEGAL NOTES

ALL RIGHTS RESERVED. NO PART OF THIS BOOK MAY BE REPRODUCED OR TRANSMITTED IN ANY FORM OR BY ANY MEANS. PHOTOCOPYING, POSTING ONLINE, AND / OR DIGITAL COPYING IS STRICTLY PROHIBITED UNLESS WRITTEN PERMISSION IS GRANTED BY THE BOOK'S PUBLISHING COMPANY. LIMITED USE OF THE BOOK'S TEXT IS PERMITTED FOR USE IN REVIEWS WRITTEN FOR THE PUBLIC.

COMMON ABBREVIATIONS

cup(s)	C.
tablespoon	tbsp
teaspoon	tsp
ounce	oz.
pound	lb

*All units used are standard American measurements

Chapter 1: Easy Veggie Burger Recipes

Summer Soy Burgers

Ingredients

- 2 tsp olive oil
- 1 small onion, grated
- 2 cloves crushed garlic
- 2 carrots, shredded
- 1 small summer squash, shredded
- 1 small zucchini, shredded
- 1 1/2 C. rolled oats
- 1/4 C. shredded Cheddar cheese
- 1 egg, beaten
- 1 tbsp soy sauce
- 1 1/2 C. all-purpose flour

Directions

- Before you do anything heat the grill and grease it.
- Place a large skillet on medium heat. Add the oil and heat it. Stir in the onion with garlic and cook them for 6 min.

- Add the carrots, squash, and zucchini then cook them for 3 min. turn off the heat. Stir in the oats, cheese, soy sauce, egg, salt and pepper.
- Get a mixing bowl: Add the veggies mix to the bowl and cover it. Place it in the fridge for 1 h 15 min. Shape the mix into 8 cakes.
- Spoon the flour into a dish. Dust the veggies burgers with flour and cook them in the grill for 6 min on each side.
- Serve your burgers with your favorite toppings.

Amount per serving 8

Timing Information:

Preparation	Enjoy.
Cooking	15 m
Total Time	20 m

Nutritional Information:

Calories	193 kcal
Fat	4.3 g
Carbohydrates	31.9g
Protein	6.9 g

* Percent Daily Values are based on a 2,000 calorie diet.

Provolone Caps Burgers

Ingredients

- 4 Portobello mushroom caps
- 1/4 C. balsamic vinegar
- 2 tbsps olive oil
- 1 tsp dried basil
- 1 tsp dried oregano
- 1 tbsp minced garlic
- Salt and pepper to taste
- 4 (1 ounce) slices provolone cheese

Directions

- Before you do anything heat the grill and grease it.
- Get a mixing bowl: Add the vinegar, oil, basil, oregano, garlic, salt, and pepper. Mix them well to make the marinade.
- Stir the mushroom into the marinade. Place it aside for 18 min. Drain the mushroom and place the marinade aside.
- Cook the mushroom caps on the grill for 7 min on each side while basting them with the marinade every 2 min. Place the cheese slices on the mushroom while it is hot to melt.
- Assemble your burgers with your favorite toppings.

- Enjoy.

Amount per serving 4

Timing Information:

Preparation	15 m
Cooking	20 m
Total Time	35 m

Nutritional Information:

Calories	203 kcal
Fat	14.6 g
Carbohydrates	9.8g
Protein	10.3 g
Cholesterol	20 mg
Sodium	259 mg

* Percent Daily Values are based on a 2,000 calorie diet.

Crunchy Cheddar Bean Burgers

Ingredients

- 1 (15 ounce) can butter beans, drained
- 1 small onion, chopped
- 1 tbsp finely chopped jalapeno pepper
- 6 saltine crackers, crushed
- 1 egg, beaten
- 1/2 C. shredded Cheddar cheese
- 1/4 tsp garlic powder
- Salt and pepper to taste
- 1/4 C. vegetable oil

Directions

- Get a mixing bowl: Add the butter beans and press them with a spoon until they become mashed.
- Add the onion, jalapeno pepper, crushed crackers, egg, cheese, garlic powder, salt, and pepper. Mix them well. Form the mix into 4 cakes.
- Place a large skillet on medium heat. Add the oil and heat it. Cook in it the butter bean cakes for 6 min per side.
- Assemble your burgers with your favorite toppings. Serve them right away.
- Enjoy.

Amount per serving 4

Timing Information:

Preparation	15 m
Cooking	10 m
Total Time	25 m

Nutritional Information:

Calories	297 kcal
Fat	20.1 g
Carbohydrates	18.5g
Protein	10.7 g
Cholesterol	61 mg
Sodium	526 mg

* Percent Daily Values are based on a 2,000 calorie diet.

Thai Bell Bean Burgers

Ingredients

- 1 (16 ounce) can black beans, drained and rinsed
- 1/2 green bell pepper, cut into 2 inch pieces
- 1/2 onion, cut into wedges
- 3 cloves garlic, peeled
- 1 egg
- 1 tbsp chili powder
- 1 tbsp cumin
- 1 tsp Thai chili sauce or hot sauce
- 1/2 C. bread crumbs

Directions

- Before you do anything heat the grill and grease it.
- Get a mixing bowl: Add the black bean then press it with a potato masher or fork until it becomes well mashed.
- Get a food processor: Add the bell pepper, onion, and garlic. Mix them well. Add the black beans and blend them smooth.
- Get a small bowl: Add the egg, chili powder, cumin, and chili sauce. Whisk them well to make the sauce. Add the black bean mix with bread crumbs. Mix them well.

- Shape the mix into 4 burger cakes. Cook them on the grill for 9 min on each side. Assemble your burgers with your favorite toppings. Serve them right away.
- Enjoy.

Amount per serving 4

Timing Information:

Preparation	15 m
Cooking	20 m
Total Time	35 m

Nutritional Information:

Calories	198 kcal
Fat	3 g
Carbohydrates	33.1g
Protein	11.2 g
Cholesterol	46 mg
Sodium	607 mg

* Percent Daily Values are based on a 2,000 calorie diet.

Latin Chili Burgers

Ingredients

- 1 carrot, sliced
- 1 (15 ounce) can kidney beans
- 1/2 C. chopped green bell pepper
- 1/2 C. chopped onion
- 2 C. salsa
- 1 C. dried bread crumbs
- 1/2 C. whole wheat flour
- 1/2 tsp ground black pepper
- Salt to taste
- 1 pinch chili powder

Directions

- Fill 1/4 inch of a heatproof bowl with water. Place the carrot on it and place on it a plastic wrap. Microwave it for 3 min. discard the water.
- Get a large mixing bowl: Add the beans with carrot. Press them with a fork or potato masher until they become smooth.
- Add the green pepper, onion, salsa, bread crumbs, and whole wheat flour, salt, black pepper, and chili powder. Mix them well. Shape the mix into 8 cakes.

- Place a large skillet on medium heat. Grease it with oil or cooking spray. Add the veggies cakes and cook them for 9 min on each side.
- Assemble your burgers with your favorite toppings. Serve them right away.
- Enjoy.

Amount per serving 8

Timing Information:

Preparation	15 m
Cooking	20 m
Total Time	35 m

Nutritional Information:

Calories	151 kcal
Fat	1.2 g
Carbohydrates	29.7g
Protein	7 g
Cholesterol	0 mg
Sodium	609 mg

* Percent Daily Values are based on a 2,000 calorie diet.

White Oyster Burgers

Ingredients

- 1 lb. fresh mushrooms, sliced
- 1 large onion, minced
- 2 slices white bread, finely diced
- 2 tbsps oyster sauce
- 1 egg
- Salt to taste
- Ground black pepper to taste

Directions

- Place a skillet on medium heat. Grease it with oil or cooking spray. Stir in the onion and mushroom then cook them for 5 min. add the bread cubes and oyster sauce. Cook them for 2 min.
- Turn off the heat. Place the mushroom mix aside to lose heat.
- Get a mixing bowl: Add the mushroom mix with egg, salt and pepper. Mix them well. Shape the mix into 6 patties. Cook them in the heated skillet for 6 min on each side.
- Assemble your burgers with your favorite toppings. Serve them right away.
- Enjoy.

Amount per serving 6

Timing Information:

Preparation	20 m
Cooking	10 m
Total Time	30 m

Nutritional Information:

Calories	61 kcal
Fat	1.4 g
Carbohydrates	9.2g
Protein	4.3 g
Cholesterol	31 mg
Sodium	110 mg

* Percent Daily Values are based on a 2,000 calorie diet.

Red Parmesan Burgers

Ingredients

- 2 tbsps vegetable oil
- 3/4 C. uncooked brown rice
- 1 1/2 C. red lentils
- 6 C. water
- 1 tsp salt
- 2 eggs
- 2 1/2 C. dry bread crumbs
- 1 1/2 C. grated Parmesan cheese
- 2 tsp dried basil
- 1 1/2 tsp garlic powder
- 3 tbsps vegetable oil

Directions

- Place a saucepan on medium heat. Add the 2 tbsps of oil and heat it. Cook the rice in it for 2 min. add the water with salt and lentils. Cook them until they start boiling.
- Lower the heat. Put on the lid. Coo them for 42 min and add more water if the mix dried before it is cooked. Place the lentils mix aside to lose heat.

- Get a food processor: Add the lentils mix with eggs, bread crumbs, Parmesan cheese, basil, and garlic powder. Pulse them several times until they become well mixed.
- Shape the mix into 16 cakes. Place a large skillet on medium heat. Heat 3 tbsps of oil in it. Add the lentils cakes and cook them for 4 min on each side.
- Assemble your burgers with your favorite toppings. Serve them right away.
- Enjoy.

Amount per serving 16

Timing Information:

Preparation	20 m
Total Time	40 m

Nutritional Information:

Calories	242 kcal
Fat	8.3 g
Carbohydrates	130.3g
Protein	11.2 g
Cholesterol	27 mg
Sodium	395 mg

* Percent Daily Values are based on a 2,000 calorie diet.

Black Seafood Burgers

Ingredients

- 1 (15 ounce) can black beans, drained and rinsed
- 1/3 C. chopped sweet onion
- 1 tbsp minced garlic
- 3 baby carrots, grated (optional)
- 1/4 C. minced green bell pepper (optional)
- 1 tbsp cornstarch
- 1 tbsp warm water
- 3 tbsps chile-garlic sauce (such as Sriracha(R)), or to taste
- 1 tsp chili powder
- 1 tsp ground cumin
- 1 tsp seafood seasoning (such as Old Bay(R))
- 1/4 tsp salt
- 1/4 tsp ground black pepper
- 2 slices whole-wheat bread, torn into small crumbs
- 3/4 C. unbleached flour, or as needed

Directions

- Before you do anything heat the oven to 350 F. Oil a baking pan.

- Get a mixing bowl: Add the black bean then press it with a potato masher or fork until it becomes well mashed. Add the onion, garlic, carrots, and green bell pepper. Combine them well.
- Get a mixing bowl: Add the cornstarch, water, chile-garlic sauce, chili powder, cumin, seafood seasoning, salt, and black pepper. Mix them well.
- Add the bean mix to the starch mix and bread crumbs. Mix them well. Shape the mix into 4 patties. Place them on the baking sheet. Cook them in the oven for 12 mi on each side.
- Assemble your burgers with your favorite toppings. Serve them right away.
- Enjoy.

Amount per serving 4

Timing Information:

Preparation	15 m
Cooking	20 m
Total Time	35 m

Nutritional Information:

Calories	264 kcal
Fat	1.4 g
Carbohydrates	51.7g
Protein	11.6 g
Cholesterol	0 mg
Sodium	1264 mg

* Percent Daily Values are based on a 2,000 calorie diet.

Korean Barbecue Burgers

Ingredients

- 1 (15.5 ounce) can garbanzo beans, drained and mashed
- 8 fresh basil leaves, chopped
- 1/4 C. oat bran
- 1/4 C. quick cooking oats
- 1 C. cooked brown rice
- 1 (14 ounce) package firm tofu
- 5 tbsps Korean barbeque sauce
- 1/2 tsp salt
- 1/2 tsp ground black pepper
- 3/4 tsp garlic powder
- 3/4 tsp dried sage
- 2 tsp vegetable oil

Directions

- Get a mixing bowl: Add the garbanzo beans and basil, oat bran, quick oats, and rice. Mix them well.
- Get a mixing bowl: Add the tofu and press it with a fork until it becomes well mashed. Drain it from the excess water that comes out of it.
- Get a mixing bowl: Add the barbecue sauce with tofu. Mix them well. Add the garbanzo mix with salt, pepper, garlic

powder, and sage. Combine them well. Shape the mix into 8 burger cakes.
- Place a large skillet on medium heat. Add the oil and heat it. Add the burger cakes and cook them for 6 min on each side.
- Assemble your burgers with your favorite toppings. Serve them right away.
- Enjoy.

Amount per serving 8

Timing Information:

Preparation	20 m
Cooking	10 m
Total Time	30 m

Nutritional Information:

Calories	161 kcal
Fat	4.7 g
Carbohydrates	23.8g
Protein	8.3 g
Cholesterol	0 mg
Sodium	340 mg

* Percent Daily Values are based on a 2,000 calorie diet.

Barbecue Cheddar Burgers

Ingredients

- 19 ounces black beans
- 1/3 C. onion, coarsely chopped
- 1 garlic clove, minced
- 1 egg
- 3 tbsps barbecue sauce or 3 tbsps ketchup
- 1 tbsp Worcestershire sauce or 1 tbsp soya sauce or 1 1/2 tsp HP steak sauce
- 1 tsp canola oil
- 1/2 tsp salt
- 1/2 tsp pepper, freshly ground
- 1/3 C. all-purpose flour
- 1/2 C. dry breadcrumbs (must be store bought to work) or 1/2 C. cracker crumb, ground in processor until very fine (must be store bought to work)
- 1/2 C. old cheddar cheese, shredded
- 6 crusty bread rolls

Directions

- Before you do anything heat the grill and grease it.
- Drain the bean. Rinse it and drain it.

- Get a food processor: Add the beans, onions, garlic, egg, 2 tbsp barbecue sauce, Worcestershire sauce, oil, salt and pepper. Pulse them until they become smooth.
- Get a mixing bowl: Add the bean mix with flour and breadcrumbs. Combine them well. Add the cheese and mix them well. Shape the mix into 6 patties.
- Spread the rest of the barbecue sauce on the bean patties. Place them in the grill and place the lid on. Cook them for 6 min on each side.
- Assemble your burgers with your favorite toppings. Serve them right away.
- Enjoy.

Amount per serving: 6

Timing Information:

Preparation	5 mins
Total Time	13 mins

Nutritional Information:

Calories	394.5
Fat	8.5g
Cholesterol	42.5mg
Sodium	1742.4mg
Carbohydrates	61.7g
Protein	217.2g

* Percent Daily Values are based on a 2,000 calorie diet.

Jack's Hickory Jalapeno Burgers

Ingredients

- 4 tbsps hickory barbecue sauce
- 1 tbsp molasses
- 1 (15 ounce) cans black beans, drained
- 2 C. cooked brown rice
- 1 tbsp oat bran
- 2 tbsps onions, finely chopped
- 1 tbsp finely chopped canned beets
- 1 tsp beet juice
- 1 tsp chili powder
- 1/4 tsp ground cumin
- 1/4 tsp black pepper
- 1 tsp kosher salt
- 1 tbsp pickled jalapeno pepper, chopped
- 1 egg white, add more if needed (to bind)
- 2 tsp olive oil
- 4 slices Monterey jack cheese (optional)

Directions

- Get a small mixing bowl: Add the barbecue sauce and molasses. Mix them gently. Place the bowl aside.

- Add the black bean then press it with a potato masher or fork until it becomes well mashed. Add the 3 tbsps of the molasses mix. Combine them well.
- Add the rice with oat bran, onion, canned beet and juice, chili powder, cumin jalapeno, egg white, salt and pepper. Mix them well. Shape the mix into 4 cakes.
- Place a large skillet on medium heat. Heat the oil in it. Add the burger cakes and cook them for 3 min. Flip the burgers then top them with the remaining molasses mix and a slice of cheese per each.
- Cook them for 3 min. Assemble your burgers with your favorite toppings. Serve them right away.
- Enjoy.

Amount per serving: 4

Timing Information:

Preparation	20 mins
Total Time	30 mins

Nutritional Information:

Calories	281.4
Fat	3.8g
Cholesterol	0.0mg
Sodium	776.5mg
Carbohydrates	52.5g
Protein	110.4g

* Percent Daily Values are based on a 2,000 calorie diet.

Quaker Corn Burgers

Ingredients

- 1 C. cooked pureed white beans, including some liquid or 1 C. beans, of your choice
- 1 C. cooked brown rice
- 1/2 C. uncooked Quaker multigrain cereal (or oats)
- 1 C. cornbread stuffing mix
- 1 tbsp parsley
- 1/2 C. chopped onion
- 1 tbsp soy sauce

Directions

- Get a mixing bowl: Add the all the ingredients. Mix them well. Shape the mix into 2 burger cakes.
- Place a skillet on medium heat. Add the oil and heat. Add the burger cakes and cook them for 5 min on each side.
- Assemble your burgers with your favorite toppings. Serve them right away.
- Enjoy.

Amount per serving: 1

Timing Information:

Preparation	15 mins
Total Time	27 mins

Nutritional Information:

Calories	112.2
Fat	0.5g
Cholesterol	0.0mg
Sodium	205.1mg
Carbohydrates	22.0g
Protein	5.2g

* Percent Daily Values are based on a 2,000 calorie diet.

Latin Salsa Burgers

Ingredients

- 1 (15 ounce) cans black beans, rinsed & drained
- 1 C. rice, cooked
- 1/4 C. onion, finely chopped
- 2 tbsps salsa
- 1 egg, beaten

Directions

- Get a mixing bowl: Add the black bean then press it with a potato masher or fork until it becomes well mashed. Add the rest of the ingredients. Mix them well. Shape the mix into 4 burger cakes.
- Place a skillet on medium heat. Add the oil and heat. Add the burger cakes and cook them for 6 min on each side.
- Assemble your burgers with your favorite toppings. Serve them right away.
- Enjoy.

Amount per serving: 4

Timing Information:

Preparation	10 mins
Total Time	20 mins

Nutritional Information:

Calories	303.8
Fat	1.9g
Cholesterol	52.8mg
Sodium	1118.0mg
Carbohydrates	59.0g
Protein	111.9g

* Percent Daily Values are based on a 2,000 calorie diet.

Hot Chili Braggs Burgers

Ingredients

- 1/4 C. onion, grated
- 1/4 C. bell pepper, grated
- 1 1/2 C. cooked lentils (or 1 15-ounce can, drained)
- 1/2 C. flax seed, ground
- 1/2 C. almonds or 1/2 C. other nuts, crushed
- 2 tbsps shredded carrots
- 2 tbsps shredded celery (remove veins with a veggie peeler)
- 1 fresh jalapenos (optional) or 1 other hot pepper, finely minced (optional)
- 2 garlic cloves, crushed
- 2 tbsps fresh parsley, chopped
- 1 tsp olive oil
- 1 tsp Braggs liquid aminos or 1 tsp soy sauce
- 1 tbsp tomato paste
- 1 tsp dried oregano
- 1 tsp dried basil
- 1/2 tsp chili powder
- 1/2 tsp curry powder
- 1/2 tsp fresh ground black pepper
- 1/4 tsp ground red pepper

Directions

- Before you do anything preheat the oven on 350 F.
- Press the bell pepper and onion in a fine masher. Press them to remove the water coming out from them.
- Get a mixing bowl: Add the 3/4 of the lentils then press it with a potato masher or fork until it becomes well mashed.
- Add the onion and pepper mix with the rest of the ingredients. Mix them well. Place the mix aside for 1 h with the lid on. Shape the mix into 6 patties.
- Place the patties on a lined up baking sheet. Cook them in the oven for 8 min on each side.
- Assemble your burgers with your favorite toppings. Serve them right away.
- Enjoy.

Amount per serving: 6

Timing Information:

Preparation	15 mins
Total Time	40 mins

Nutritional Information:

Calories	219.3
Fat	12.9g
Cholesterol	0.0mg
Sodium	74.4mg
Carbohydrates	19.1g
Protein	9.9g

* Percent Daily Values are based on a 2,000 calorie diet.

Peanut Butter Burgers

Ingredients

- 1 C. textured vegetable protein
- 1/4 C. quick-cooking rolled oats
- 1/2 tsp dried oregano
- 1/2 tsp dried basil, flakes
- 1/2 tsp dried parsley flakes
- 1/2 tsp onion, granules
- 1/2 tsp garlic granules
- 1/4 tsp mustard powder
- 3/4 C. water (almost-boiling)
- 2 tbsps organic ketchup
- 2 tbsps soy sauce (or tamari or Bragg's)
- 1 tbsp creamy peanut butter (can also use tahini or any other nut or seed butter)
- 1/4 C. whole wheat pastry flour
- 1 tbsp nutritional yeast

Directions

- Get a mixing bowl: Add the water with oregano, basil, parsley flakes, onion, garlic granules, and mustard powder, oats and TVP chunks. Combine them well.

- Stir in the ketchup and soy sauce. Mix them well. Fold in the nut butter with whole-wheat pastry flour and nutritional yeast. Combine them well. Shape the mix into 4 burger cakes.
- Place a large skillet on medium heat. Heat in it a splash of oil. Add the burgers and cook them for 7 min on each side.
- Assemble your burgers with your favorite toppings. Serve them right away.
- Enjoy.

Amount per serving: 4

Timing Information:

Preparation	10 mins
Total Time	25 mins

Nutritional Information:

Calories	93.4
Fat	2.8g
Cholesterol	0.0mg
Sodium	608.6mg
Carbohydrates	13.7g
Protein	5.1g

* Percent Daily Values are based on a 2,000 calorie diet.

Braggs' Oat Burgers

Ingredients

- 1 tbsp extra virgin olive oil
- 1/2 C. onion, finely chopped
- 1/4 C. grated carrot
- 1/4 C. celery, finely chopped
- 1/4 C. grated zucchini or 1/4 C. summer squash
- 1 C. cooked brown rice
- 1 1/2 C. quick oats
- 1/2 tsp garlic powder
- 1/2 tsp cumin powder
- 1/8 tsp cayenne powder
- 1 tbsp nutritional yeast flakes
- 1 (12 1/3 ounce) packages firm tofu or 1 (12 1/3 ounce) packages extra firm tofu
- 1 tsp all-purpose vegetable
- 1/2 C. water
- 2 tbsps Braggs liquid aminos or 2 tbsps soy sauce
- Breadcrumbs, for coating the patties

Directions

- Before you do anything preheat the oven on 375 F.

- Place a large skillet on medium heat. Heat the olive oil in it. Add the onion, carrot, celery and zucchini then cook them for 5 min. Turn off the heat.
- Stir in the rice, oats and seasonings. Combine them well. Stir in the tofu and press it with a fork until it becomes finely mashed.
- Get a mixing bowl: Add the water with aminos. Mix them well. Add the tofu mix and combine them well. Shape the mix into 8 burger cakes. Coat them with the bread crumbs.
- Place the burgers on a lined up baking sheet. Cook them in the oven for 16 min. Flip them and grease them with a cooking spray. Cook them for 22 min. Let them rest for 6 min.
- Assemble your burgers with your favorite toppings. Serve them right away.
- Enjoy.

Amount per serving: 8

Timing Information:

Preparation	20 mins
Total Time	1 hr.

Nutritional Information:

Calories	143.3
Fat	4.8g
Cholesterol	0.0mg
Sodium	13.0mg
Carbohydrates	18.9g
Protein	7.4g

* Percent Daily Values are based on a 2,000 calorie diet.

Chili Romano Burgers

Ingredients

- 1 (19 ounce) cans Romano beans or 1 (19 ounce) cans white kidney beans, drained & rinsed
- 1 egg
- 1/2 C. dry breadcrumbs
- 1/4 C. chili sauce or 1/4 C. salsa or 1/4 C. mango chutney
- 1 green onion, chopped

Directions

- Add the 3/4 of the black bean then press it with a potato masher or fork until it becomes well mashed. Add the rest of the ingredients. Mix them well. Shape the mix into 4 burger cakes.
- Place a large skillet on medium heat. Add the oil and heat it. Cook the burgers for 7 min on each side.
- Assemble your burgers with your favorite toppings. Serve them right away.
- Enjoy.

Amount per serving: 4

Timing Information:

Preparation	10 mins
Total Time	20 mins

Nutritional Information:

Calories	110.3
Fat	2.1g
Cholesterol	46.5mg
Sodium	1694.2mg
Carbohydrates	18.1g
Protein	4.9g

* Percent Daily Values are based on a 2,000 calorie diet.

Curry Nuts Burgers

Ingredients

- 1 C. shelled raw walnuts
- 1 C. raw cashews
- 1 C. raw sunflower seeds
- 1 C. shelled raw almonds
- 1 C. chopped celery
- 1 C. carrot, pulp (leftover after making carrot juice)
- 1 C. chopped onion
- 2 -3 cloves minced garlic
- 1 tbsp chopped parsley
- 1 1/2 tbsps minced sage
- 1/2 C. whey powder
- 2 large eggs
- 1/4 tsp mustard powder
- 1/4 tsp curry powder
- 1 tsp poultry seasoning
- 1 tsp ground cumin
- 1 tsp mild chili powder
- 2 -3 tbsps olive oil (for frying burgers)

Directions

- Get a food processor: Add the walnuts, cashews, sunflower seeds, almonds, celery, carrot pulp, onion, garlic cloves, parsley, and sage. Process them several times until they become finely chopped.
- Get a mixing bowl: Add the nuts mix with whey powder, eggs, dry mustard powder, curry powder, poultry seasoning, cumin, and mild chili powder. Mix them well. Shape the mix into 6 large burger cakes.
- Place a large skillet on medium heat. Heat the oil in it. Add the burgers and cook them for 6 min on each side.
- Assemble your burgers with your favorite toppings. Serve them right away.
- Enjoy.

Amount per serving: 6

Timing Information:

Preparation	20 mins
Total Time	40 mins

Nutritional Information:

Calories	670.5
Fat	56.0g
Cholesterol	862.0mg
Sodium	2411.7mg
Carbohydrates	34.1g
Protein	121.3g

* Percent Daily Values are based on a 2,000 calorie diet.

White Steak Burgers

Ingredients

- 1 lb. fresh mushrooms, about 6 C. chopped finely
- 1 large onion, minced
- 2 slices white bread, finely diced
- 2 tbsps steak sauce
- 2 egg whites or 1 egg
- Salt
- Ground black pepper

Directions

- Place a large skillet on medium heat. Grease it with oil or cooking spray. Add the onion with mushroom and sauté them for 6 min. Add the bread dices with steak sauce. Sauté them for 1 min
- Turn off the heat. Place the mix aside to lose heat.
- Get a mixing bowl: Add the eggs and mix them well. Add the onion mix with salt and pepper. Mix them well. Shape the mix into 6 burgers.
- Place a large skillet on medium heat. Heat in it a splash of oil. Add the burgers and cook them for 8 min on each side.

- Assemble your burgers with your favorite toppings. Serve them right away.
- Enjoy.

Amount per serving: 6

Timing Information:

Preparation	20 mins
Total Time	30 mins

Nutritional Information:

Calories	54.5
Fat	0.5g
Cholesterol	0.0mg
Sodium	65.6mg
Carbohydrates	9.1g
Protein	4.4g

* Percent Daily Values are based on a 2,000 calorie diet.

Rolled Kidney Bean Burgers

Ingredients

- 2 C. red kidney beans, drained, rinsed (from 19-oz can)
- 1/2 C. uncooked rolled oats
- 1/2 C. chopped fresh mushrooms
- 1/4 C. chopped onion
- 1 small carrot, shredded
- 1/2 medium red bell pepper, chopped
- 1 garlic clove, minced
- 2 tbsps ketchup
- 3/4 tsp salt
- 4 lettuce leaves
- 4 slices tomatoes
- 4 hamburger buns split

Directions

- Before you do anything preheat the oven broiler.
- Get a food processor: Add the beans, oats, mushrooms, onion, carrot, bell pepper, garlic, ketchup and salt. Mix them well until they become chopped. Form the mix into 4 burgers.
- Grease a baking sheet. Place the burgers on it. Cook it in the oven broiler for 7 min on each side.

- Assemble your burgers starting with a bun, lettuce, tomato, burger, ketchup and bun. Serve them right away.
- Enjoy.

Amount per serving: 1

Timing Information:

Preparation	15 mins
Total Time	27 mins

Nutritional Information:

Calories	301.9
Fat	3.1g
Cholesterol	0.0mg
Sodium	745.2mg
Carbohydrates	55.2g
Protein	114.6g

* Percent Daily Values are based on a 2,000 calorie diet.

Tamari Burger Casserole

Ingredients

- 2 tbsps olive oil
- 1 large yellow onion, chopped
- 1 large carrot, chopped
- 4 ounces white mushrooms, chopped
- 1 tbsp tomato paste
- 2 tbsps tamari or 2 tbsps other soy sauce
- 1 C. of basic vegetable broth
- 1 tsp minced fresh thyme
- 1 tsp minced fresh marjoram
- Salt & fresh ground pepper
- 1 tbsp cornstarch, dissolved in
- 2 tbsps water
- 3 frozen veggie burgers, thawed and crumbled
- 1/2 C. frozen green pea
- 1/4 C. ground walnuts
- 3 C. mashed potatoes (try a mix of Yukon and sweet potatoes or squash & parsnips)
- 1/4 tsp paprika

Directions

- Before you do anything preheat the oven to 375 F. Grease a casserole dish. Place it aside.
- Place a lire skillet on medium heat. Add 1 tbsp of olive oil. Stir in the carrot with onion. Put on the lid and cook them for 6 min. Stir in the mushroom. Cook them for 4 min.
- Add the tomato paste, tamari, veggie stock, thyme, marjoram, cornstarch mix, salt and pepper. Simmer them for 2 min. Fold in the burgers with walnuts and peas, seasonings, salt and pepper.
- Lay the burger mix in the casserole. Lay on it the potato then top it with paprika and the rest of the olive oil.
- Cook the burger casserole in the oven for 34 min. serve your burger casserole right away.
- Enjoy.

Amount per serving: 6

Timing Information:

Preparation	40 mins
Total Time	1 hr. 10 mins

Nutritional Information:

Calories	258.2
Fat	9.7g
Cholesterol	3.8mg
Sodium	907.3mg
Carbohydrates	33.1g
Protein	110.9g

* Percent Daily Values are based on a 2,000 calorie diet.

Sea Lentils Burgers

Ingredients

- 1 C. lentils (dry measure)
- 1 onion, diced
- 3 carrots, grated
- 3/4 C. whole grain flour (approx.)
- 1 pinch sea salt
- 1 tsp coriander
- 1 tsp cumin
- 1/4 tsp cayenne pepper
- 1 pinch black pepper
- 1 -2 tsp olive oil

Directions

- Bring a salted pot of water to a boil. Add the lentils and cook it until it is done. Drain it.
- Get a mixing bowl: Add the carrot with onion and lentils then press them slightly with a fork to mash them a bit. Add the flour with seasoning, salt and pepper then mix them well.
- Place a large skillet on medium heat. Add the olive oil and heat it. Shape the lentils mix into 3 burgers. Cook them in the heated skillet for 9 min on each side.

- Assemble your burgers with your favorite toppings. Serve them right away.
- Enjoy.

Amount per serving: 3

Timing Information:

Preparation	10 mins
Total Time	1 hr.

Nutritional Information:

Calories	248.8
Fat	2.4g
Cholesterol	0.0mg
Sodium	240.7mg
Carbohydrates	47.4g
Protein	110.4g

* Percent Daily Values are based on a 2,000 calorie diet.

Beasty Garbanzo Burgers

Ingredients

- 1 carrot (medium size grated)
- 1 garlic clove
- 1 (19 ounce) cans chickpeas
- 1 1/2 tsp ground cumin
- 1 1/2 tsp ground coriander
- Salt & pepper
- 1 large egg
- 2 tbsps plain flour
- Oil (for frying)
- 2 slices whole wheat bread (cut in round shapes)
- 1 tomato
- 1 red onion

Directions

- Chop the garlic. Grate the carrot.
- Get a food processor: Add the chickpea with spices, garlic, salt and pepper. Pulse them several times until they become smooth. Add the carrot, egg, and flour. Process them again.

- Place a large skillet on medium heat. Heat the oil in it. Shape the chickpea mix into 8 patties and cook them for 4 min on each side. Toast the bread.
- Assemble your burgers with the tomato and onion slices and your favorite toppings. Serve them right away.
- Enjoy.

Amount per serving: 8

Timing Information:

Preparation	10 mins
Total Time	25 mins

Nutritional Information:

Calories	127.6
Fat	23.2mg
Cholesterol	250.7mg
Sodium	22.6g
Carbohydrates	5.7g
Protein	100.4g

* Percent Daily Values are based on a 2,000 calorie diet.

Balsamic Mayo Burgers

Ingredients

- 4 large Portobello mushroom caps
- 1/2 C. soy sauce
- 1/2 C. balsamic vinegar
- 4 cloves garlic, chopped, or more to taste
- 1 large red bell pepper
- 1 C. reduced-fat mayonnaise
- 1 tbsp cayenne pepper, or to taste
- 4 hamburger buns split

Directions

- Get a zip lock bag: Add the mushroom with soy sauce, balsamic vinegar, and garlic. Shake the bag roughly to coat the ingredients. Place it aside for 2 h 30 min.
- Before you do anything heat the grill and grease it.
- Cook the bell pepper for 6 min on each side. Drain the mushroom caps from the marinade and cook them for 7 min on each side.
- Transfer the bell pepper to a zip lock bag and seal it and place them aside for 5 min sweat. Peel the bell peppers and chop them.

- Get a mixing bowl: Add the roasted bell pepper with mayo and cayenne pepper. Mix them well. Place it in the fridge until ready to serve.
- Assemble your burgers with your favorite toppings. Serve them right away.
- Enjoy.

Amount per serving 4

Timing Information:

Preparation	15 m
Cooking	15 m
Total Time	2 h 40 m

Nutritional Information:

Calories	375 kcal
Fat	22.5 g
Carbohydrates	337.8g
Protein	7.1 g
Cholesterol	21 mg
Sodium	2459 mg

* Percent Daily Values are based on a 2,000 calorie diet.

Parmesan Kernels Burger

Ingredients

- 2 ounces olive oil
- 3 tbsps diced red onions
- 2 tbsps diced black olives
- 2 tbsps diced red bell peppers
- 1/2 potato, boiled
- 3 tbsps sweet whole kernel corn
- 1 tsp diced jalapeno
- 1 1/2 tbsps diced garlic
- 4 ounces black beans, drained
- 4 ounces kidney beans, drained
- 4 ounces white beans, drained
- 1/2 tsp chili powder
- 1 tsp dried oregano
- 1 tbsp minced fresh parsley leaves
- 1 tsp red chili pepper flakes
- 1/2 tsp ground cumin
- 1 tsp celery salt
- 1/4 tsp ground sage
- 2 tbsps seasoned bread crumbs
- 1/4 C. grated parmesan cheese
- 1 egg

Directions

- Bring a salted pot of water to a boil. Add the potato and cook it until it becomes soft. Place it aside to lose heat.
- Place a large skillet. Add 1 ounce of oil and cook in it the onion with bell peppers and jalapeno. Cook them for 5 min. Place the mix aside to lose heat.
- Stir in half of the cooked potato with black, kidney and white beans. Mix them well. Stir in the remaining ingredients. Mix them well. Shape the mix into 4 burgers. Place them in the fridge for 5 min.
- Place a large skillet on medium heat. Add the burgers and cook them for 4 min on each side. Assemble your burgers with your favorite toppings. Serve them right away.
- Enjoy.

Amount per serving: 4
Timing Information:

Preparation	45 mins
Total Time	50 mins

Nutritional Information:

Calories	313.3
Fat	18.5g
Cholesterol	252.0mg
Sodium	1338.7mg
Carbohydrates	27.1g
Protein	11.2g

* Percent Daily Values are based on a 2,000 calorie diet.

Baby Cheddar Burger

Ingredients

- 1 kg potato, peeled
- 200 g of grated cheddar cheese
- 800 g frozen mixed vegetables (or fresh if you prefer)
- 1 Spanish onion
- 250 g golden breadcrumbs
- Salt and pepper

Directions

- Before you do anything preheat the oven to 400 F. Grease an oven proof grilling pan.
- Bring a salted pot of water to a boil. Add the potato and cook it until it becomes soft. Place it aside to lose heat then mash it.
- Get a mixing bowl: Add the mashed potato with onion, cheese, mixed veggies, salt and pepper. Divide the mix into 5 portions. Ask your kids to add mix them with their hands.
- Shape them into burgers. Place a grill pan on medium heat. Place the burgers on the pan. Cook them in the oven for 20 min on each side.

- Assemble your burgers with yours ad your kids' favorite toppings. Serve them right away.
- Enjoy.

Amount per serving: 5

Timing Information:

Preparation	45 mins
Total Time	45 mins

Nutritional Information:

Calories	624.1
Fat	16.9g
Cholesterol	242.0mg
Sodium	1702.9mg
Carbohydrates	95.0g
Protein	326.2g

* Percent Daily Values are based on a 2,000 calorie diet.

Nutty Teriyaki Burges

Ingredients

- 1/2 tbsp peanut oil
- 1/2 C. onion (purple)
- 1 C. zucchini
- 1/2 C. red bell pepper
- 2 eggs
- 1/2 tsp ginger (ground)
- 1/2 tsp cumin
- 1/4 C. soy sauce
- 1/4 C. teriyaki sauce
- 1/4 C. walnut pieces
- 1 1/2 C. brown rice (cooked)

Directions

- Before you do anything heat the oven on 350 F.
- Chop the bell pepper with zucchini until they become fine. Mince the onion.
- Place a large skillet on medium heat. Add the oil and heat it. Stir in the onion and cook it for 6 min.
- Stir in the chopped zucchini with bell pepper to the onion. Cook them for 16 min while stirring occasionally. Turn off the heat and allow the mix to lose heat.

- Get a mixing bowl: Add the eggs and beat them. Stir in the onion mix with ginger, cumin, soy sauce, teriyaki sauce, walnuts and cooked rice. Mix them well. Shape the mix into 4 burgers.
- Place the burgers on the baking pan. Cook them in the oven for 8 min on each side.
- Assemble your burgers with your favorite toppings. Serve them right away.
- Enjoy.

Amount per serving: 4

Timing Information:

Preparation	30 mins
Total Time	45 mins

Nutritional Information:

Calories	402.7
Fat	11.1g
Cholesterol	93.0mg
Sodium	31740.4mg
Carbohydrates	62.8g
Protein	213.5g

* Percent Daily Values are based on a 2,000 calorie diet.

Farmer's Market Burger

Ingredients

- 2 whole eggplants, peeled, diced into 1-inch cubes (about 1 lb. each, you can leave peel on)
- 1 tbsp butter (or margarine)
- 2 -3 scallions, chopped fine
- 1 tbsp parsley, minced (also good with cilantro)
- 1 C. shredded cheddar cheese (medium recommended- can use goat cheese or feta)
- 1 C. breadcrumbs (one reviewer used gluten free cracker crumbs)
- 3/4 tsp fresh ground black pepper
- 1 tsp garlic, minced
- 1/4 tsp salt
- 3 tbsps olive oil

Directions

- Place a large skillet on medium heat. Add 1 tbsp of butter and cook it until it melts. Add the eggplant dices and cook them for 8 min on each side.
- Get a mixing bowl: Add the cooked eggplant with the scallions, parsley, cheese, breadcrumbs, garlic, salt and

pepper. Combine them well. Place the mix in the fridge for 35 min.
- Shape the mix into 4 burgers. Place a large skillet on medium heat. Add the oil and heat it. Cook in it the burgers for 6 min on each side.
- Assemble your burgers with your favorite toppings. Serve them right away.
- Enjoy.

Amount per serving: 1

Timing Information:

Preparation	20 mins
Total Time	45 mins

Nutritional Information:

Calories	281.4
Fat	14.9g
Cholesterol	27.6mg
Sodium	375.0mg
Carbohydrates	33.6g
Protein	16.2g

* Percent Daily Values are based on a 2,000 calorie diet.

Saucy Vegan Burger

Ingredients

- 1/2 C. chili sauce
- 1 tbsp Worcestershire sauce
- 1/4 tsp dried thyme, crushed
- 1/8 tsp cayenne pepper
- 2 frozen veggie burgers (3.2 oz. each)
- 1/4 tsp dried garlic
- 1/4 tsp ground black pepper
- Lettuce leaf
- Red onion, slices
- Fresh chives, snipped

Directions

- Before you do anything heat the grill and grease it.
- Get a small saucepan: Add the chili sauce, Worcestershire sauce, thyme and red pepper.
- Mix them well and bring them to a boil to make the sauce. Lower the heat and cook the sauce for 4 min.
- Place the burgers on the grill and cook them for 3 min on each side. Season the burgers with black pepper and garlic on both sides. Cook them for 2 min on each side.

- Assemble your burgers with your favorite toppings. Serve them right away.
- Enjoy.

Amount per serving: 2

Timing Information:

Preparation	5 mins
Total Time	11 mins

Nutritional Information:

Calories	202.6
Fat	4.6g
Cholesterol	3.5mg
Sodium	1395.0mg
Carbohydrates	25.6g
Protein	12.7g

* Percent Daily Values are based on a 2,000 calorie diet.

Chili Corn Burgers

Ingredients

- 1 carrot, sliced
- 1 (15 ounce) cans garbanzo beans
- 2 C. store-brand fresh salsa
- 1 C. crushed corn flakes
- 1/2 C. whole wheat flour
- 1/2 tsp fresh pepper
- Salt
- 1 pinch chili powder

Directions

- Fill 1/4 inch of a bowl with water. Add the carrot. Cook it in the microwave for 3 min. discard the water.
- Get a mixing bowl: Add the beans with carrot. Press them with a fork until they become finely mashed. Add the salsa with corn flakes, flour, salt, chili powder and pepper. Mix them well.
- Shape the mix into 8 burgers. Grease a skillet and put it on medium heat. Add the burgers and cook them for 9 min on each side.
- Assemble your burgers with your favorite toppings. Serve them right away.

- Enjoy.

Amount per serving: 8

Timing Information:

Preparation	5 mins
Total Time	21 mins

Nutritional Information:

Calories	124.7
Fat	1.0g
Cholesterol	0.0mg
Sodium	586.3mg
Carbohydrates	25.8g
Protein	5.0g

* Percent Daily Values are based on a 2,000 calorie diet.

Nuts Burger

Ingredients

- 1 C. chopped onion
- 2 tbsps minced garlic
- 1 tbsp olive oil
- 3 tbsps chopped fresh basil or 2 tsp dried basil
- 2 C. cooked brown rice
- 1/3 C. cashews
- 1/3 C. walnuts
- 1/3 C. almonds
- 1/3 C. sunflower seeds
- 1/4 C. tamari soy sauce
- 2/3 C. tahini

Directions

- Place a skillet on medium heat. Heat half tbsp of oil in it. Add the onion and cook it for 4 min. Stir in the basil with rice and mix them well.
- Get a food processor! Add the sunflower seeds with cashews, walnuts and almonds. Process them until they become finely chopped.
- Spoon the chopped nuts to the rice with tamari and tahini. Mix them well. Form the mix into 6 burgers.

- Place a large skillet on medium heat. Heat in it half tbsp of oil Add the burgers and cook them for 6 min on each side.
- Assemble your burgers with your favorite toppings. Serve them right away.
- Enjoy.

Amount per serving: 6

Timing Information:

Preparation	15 mins
Total Time	25 mins

Nutritional Information:

Calories	444.2
Fat	31.4g
Cholesterol	40.0mg
Sodium	781.2mg
Carbohydrates	32.9g
Protein	113.4g

* Percent Daily Values are based on a 2,000 calorie diet.

Chipotle Cannellini Burgers

Ingredients

- 2 C. cooked red quinoa
- 1 C. cannellini beans, mashed
- 1/2 C. panko breadcrumbs
- 1 large egg, lightly beaten
- 1 garlic clove, grated
- 1 tsp dried chipotle powder
- 1/2 tsp salt
- 1/2 tsp pepper
- 3/4 C. sharp cheddar cheese, shredded
- 3 tbsps olive oil
- 4 your favorite hamburger buns

Directions

- Get a mixing bowl: Add the quinoa, mashed cannellini beans, bread crumbs, egg, garlic, chipotle chili powder, salt and pepper. Combine them well. Add the cheese and combine them well.
- Shape the mix into 5 cakes and refrigerate it for 5 min.
- Place a large skillet on medium heat. Heat 1 tbsp of oil in it. Add the cakes and cook them for 6 min on each side. Place a slice of cheese of cheese on each cake.

- Put on the lid and cook them for 2 min until the cheese melts. Assemble your burgers with your favorite toppings. Serve them right away.
- Enjoy.

Amount per serving: 5

Timing Information:

Preparation	30 mins
Total Time	45 mins

Nutritional Information:

Calories	427.6
Fat	18.5g
Cholesterol	255.0mg
Sodium	1761.7mg
Carbohydrates	48.8g
Protein	116.2g

* Percent Daily Values are based on a 2,000 calorie diet.

Red Pecans Burgers

Ingredients

- 1 C. water
- 1/2 C. red quinoa
- 1 tbsp oil (of your choice)
- 1 C. onion, diced
- 2 C. mushrooms, finely chopped
- 1 garlic clove, minced
- 1 tsp Italian seasoning
- 1/2 tsp salt
- 1/4 tsp pepper
- 1 egg
- 3 tbsps cornstarch
- 1/2 C. whole pecans, toasted and finely chopped
- 1 tbsp gluten-free soy sauce
- 2/3 C. gluten-free fat-free cheddar cheese
- 1/3 C. gluten-free quick-cooking rolled oats

Directions

- Before you do anything preheat the oven on 350 F.
- Place a saucepan on medium heat. Stir in the quinoa and cook it until it starts boiling. Lower the heat and put on the lid. Cook them for 16 min.

- Turn off the heat and place the quinoa aside to rest for 8 min. Mix it gently with a fork.
- Lay the pecans on a lined up baking sheet. Cook it in the oven for 8 min.
- Place a large skillet on medium heat. Add oil and heat it. Stir in the onion and cook it for 4 min. Stir in the mushrooms, garlic, and spices. Cook them for 6 min.
- Place the onion mix aside to lose heat. Get a mixing bowl: Add the egg and mix it well. Stir in the quinoa, mushroom and the rest of the ingredients.
- Shape the mix into 6 burgers. Place the burgers on a lined up baking sheet. Cook them in the oven for 32 min. assemble your burgers with your favorite toppings. Serve them right away.
- Enjoy.

Amount per serving: 6

Timing Information:

Preparation	30 mins
Total Time	1 hr.

Nutritional Information:

Calories	190.1
Fat	10.2g
Cholesterol	31.0mg
Sodium	1210.4mg
Carbohydrates	20.4g
Protein	5.4g

* Percent Daily Values are based on a 2,000 calorie diet.

Bell Artichoke Burgers

Ingredients

- 2 (15 ounce) cans garbanzo beans, drained and rinsed
- 1 small onion, chopped
- 6 garlic cloves, chopped
- 1/2 C. red bell pepper, chopped
- 1/3 C. Kalamata olive, chopped
- 1 (8 ounce) jars marinated artichokes, drained and chopped
- 2 C. spinach, chopped (fresh)
- 1/2 C. oats
- 1/2 tsp dried oregano
- 1/4 tsp salt
- 1/4 tsp pepper
- 1/2 C. breadcrumbs

Directions

- Get a mixing bowl: Add the beans, onion, and garlic. Press them with a fork and mash them for a bit. Stir in the remaining ingredients and mix them well.
- Shape the mix into 6 burgers. Place a large skillet on medium heat and grease it. Cook in it the burgers for 6 min on each side.

- Assemble your burgers with your favorite toppings. Serve them right away.
- Enjoy.

Amount per serving: 6

Timing Information:

Preparation	15 mins
Total Time	25 mins

Nutritional Information:

Calories	299.1
Fat	4.0g
Cholesterol	0.0mg
Sodium	673.8mg
Carbohydrates	55.4g
Protein	112.3g

* Percent Daily Values are based on a 2,000 calorie diet.

Hollywood Burgers

Ingredients

- 2 tbsps olive oil
- 1 small yellow onion, chopped
- 1/2 small yellow bell pepper, chopped
- 1 (15 1/2 ounce) cans chickpeas, drained and rinsed (or 1 1/2 c. cooked)
- 3/4 tsp salt
- 1/4 tsp fresh ground black pepper
- 1/4 C. wheat gluten flour
- 4 burger rolls

Directions

- Place a large skillet on medium heat. Add 1 tbsp oil in it. Stir in the onion pepper and cook them for 6 min. Place the mix aside to lose heat.
- Get a food processor: Add the onion mix with chickpeas, salt, and pepper. Process them until they become smooth. Stir in the flour and combine them well. Shape the mix into 4 burgers.
- Place a large skillet on medium heat. Heat in it 1 tbsp of olive oil Add the burgers and cook them for 6 min on each side.

- Assemble your burgers with your favorite toppings. Serve them right away.
- Enjoy.

Amount per serving: 4

Timing Information:

Preparation	30 mins
Total Time	40 mins

Nutritional Information:

Calories	397.5
Fat	10.6g
Cholesterol	0.0mg
Sodium	1078.0mg
Carbohydrates	58.8g
Protein	117.1g

* Percent Daily Values are based on a 2,000 calorie diet.

Chili Mexican Black Bean Burgers

Ingredients

- 1/2 C. brown rice, uncooked
- 1 C. water
- 2 (16 ounce) cans black beans, rinsed and drained
- 1 green bell pepper, halved and seeded
- 1 onion, quartered
- 1/2 C. mushroom, sliced
- 6 garlic cloves, peeled
- 3/4 C. mozzarella cheese, shredded
- 2 eggs
- 1 tbsp chili powder
- 1 tbsp ground cumin
- 1 tbsp garlic salt
- 1 tsp hot sauce
- 1/2 C. dry breadcrumbs, as needed

DIRECTIONS

- Before you do anything heat the grill and grease it.
- Cook the rice according to the directions on the package. Place it aside to lose the heat. Fluff it with a fork.
- Get a mixing bowl: Add the black bean then press it with a potato masher or fork until it becomes well mashed.

- Get a food processor: Add the bell pepper, onion, mushrooms, and garlic. Pulse them several times until they become finely chopped.
- Add the onion mix to the mashed bean and combine them well.
- Get a food processor: Add the rice with mozzarella cheese. Pulse them several times until they become well combined. Add them to the bean mix and combine them well.
- Get a mixing bowl: Add the eggs, chili powder, cumin, garlic salt, and hot sauce. Mix them well. Add the black bean mix and combine them well.
- Add the breadcrumbs and mix them again. Shape the mix into 6 burgers. Cook them in the grill for 9 min on each side. Assemble your burgers with your favorite toppings. Serve them right away.
- Enjoy.

Amount per serving: 6

Timing Information:

Preparation	25 mins
Total Time	40 mins

Nutritional Information:

Calories	332.5
Fat	6.7g
Cholesterol	73.0mg
Sodium	2228.0mg
Carbohydrates	50.8g
Protein	118.6g

* Percent Daily Values are based on a 2,000 calorie diet.

Amaranth Millet Burgers

Ingredients

- 1 1/2 C. water
- 1/2 C. millet, dry
- 2 garlic cloves, minced
- 2 tbsps raw coconut oil
- 1 onion, large minced
- 3 C. spinach, finely chopped
- 2 celery ribs, finely chopped
- 2 carrots, peeled minced
- 2 tsp sea salt
- 1 tbsp cumin
- 1/2 tsp black pepper
- 1 C. amaranth flour

Directions

- Cook the millet according to the instructions on the package. Use a food processor to the shred celery, spinach and carrot.
- Place a large skillet on medium heat. Add 1 tbsp of coconut oil and heat it. Add the onion and cook it for 4 min. Stir in the celery with spinach, salt and carrot. Cook them for 6 min.

- Remove the skillet from the heat. Add the flour and mix them well. Place the mix aside to lose heat. Shape the mix into 6 burgers.
- Place a large skillet on medium heat. Add the remaining oil and heat it. Cook the burgers in it for 6 min on each side. Assemble your burgers with your favorite toppings. Serve them right away.
- Enjoy.

Amount per serving: 6

Timing Information:

Preparation	24 hrs.
Total Time	24 hrs. 20 mins

Nutritional Information:

Calories	190.8
Fat	6.7g
Cholesterol	0.0mg
Sodium	817.6mg
Carbohydrates	28.5g
Protein	5.2g

* Percent Daily Values are based on a 2,000 calorie diet.

Juicy Beet Burgers

Ingredients

- 1 1/4 C. cooked brown rice, cooled
- 1 C. cooked lentils, cooled
- 1 C. beet, peeled and shredded
- 1/2 tsp salt
- Fresh ground black pepper, to taste
- 1 tsp dried thyme
- 1/2 tsp ground fennel
- 1 tsp dry mustard
- 3 tbsps onions, minced
- 2 garlic cloves, minced
- 1 egg
- 1/2 C. fine dry breadcrumb
- 1 tbsp olive oil
- 4 whole wheat buns, toasted
- Condiments, as desired

Directions

- Get a food processor: Add the lentils with rice and beer. Process them for 1 min until they become lean.
- Get a mixing bowl: Add the rice mix with salt, pepper, thyme, fennel, mustard, onion, garlic, egg and bread

crumbs. Mix them well. Place it in the fridge for 3 h. Shape the mix into 4 patties.
- Place a large skillet on medium heat. Add the oil and heat it. Cook in it the burgers for 7 min on each side. Assemble your burgers with your favorite toppings. Serve them right away.
- Enjoy.

Amount per serving: 4

Timing Information:

Preparation	5 hrs.
Total Time	5 hrs 15 mins

Nutritional Information:

Calories	368.1
Fat	8.8g
Cholesterol	46.5mg
Sodium	1639.6mg
Carbohydrates	59.2g
Protein	114.4g

* Percent Daily Values are based on a 2,000 calorie diet.

Sweet and Spicy Burger

Ingredients

- 2 ounces olive oil
- 6 tbsps diced red onions
- 4 tbsps diced black olives
- 5 tbsps diced red peppers
- 4 tbsps diced garlic
- 4 ounces black beans, rinsed and drained
- 4 ounces white beans, rinsed and drained
- 4 ounces chickpeas, rinsed and drained
- 8 ounces rolled oats
- 2 tbsps southwest jalapeno dip mix (gourmetcreations.net)
- 2 tbsps minced fresh parsley leaves
- 1/2 tsp celery salt
- 4 tbsps seasoned bread crumbs or 4 tbsps panko breadcrumbs
- 1 egg

Directions

- Place a skillet on medium heat. Add the oil and heat it. Add the onion with bell pepper and garlic. Cook them for 6 min. Place the mix aside to lose heat.

- Cook the rolled oats according to the directions on the package. Place it aside to lose it heat. Mash it slightly with a fork.
- Get a mixing bowl: Add the remaining ingredients and combine them well. Stir in the onion mix with oatmeal and combine them well. Shape the mix into 4 burgers. Place them in the fridge for 35 min.
- Place a large skillet on medium heat. Heat the oil in it. Add the burgers and cook them for 5 min on each side. Assemble your burgers with your favorite toppings. Serve them right away.
- Enjoy.

Amount per serving: 4

Timing Information:

Preparation	45 mins
Total Time	55 mins

Nutritional Information:

Calories	512.3
Fat	20.9g
Cholesterol	346.5mg
Sodium	1305.0mg
Carbohydrates	66.4g
Protein	216.3g

* Percent Daily Values are based on a 2,000 calorie diet.

Late October Tahini Burgers

Ingredients

- 1 1/2 C. pumpkin puree
- 8 ounces silken tofu, well-drained (see directions)
- 1 tbsp tahini (thicker tahini works best)
- 2 egg whites (or 1 whole egg)
- 2 green onions
- 1/3 C. raw pepitas (the green hulled unsalted unroasted kind)
- 1 tbsp whole sage, dry
- 1 tsp coriander
- 1/2 tsp dried thyme
- 1 dash white pepper (a few shakes)
- 1 pinch ginger powder
- 1 C. rolled oats (or as much needed to hold together)

Directions

- Remove the tofu from the excess water. Place it in a colander for 5 min to drain it.
- Get a mixing bowl: Add the tofu with pumpkin, tahini, and egg whites. Use an electric mix to mix them until they become smooth. Add the sage with spices. Combine them well.

- Add the green onions with pepitas and 1 C. of cooked oats. Mix them well and add more oat if needed. Shape the mix into 6 patties.
- Place a large skillet on medium heat. Heat the oil in it. Add the burgers and cook them for 5 min on each side. Assemble your burgers with your favorite toppings. Serve them right away.
- Enjoy.

Amount per serving: 6

Timing Information:

Preparation	10 mins
Total Time	35 mins

Nutritional Information:

Calories	142.5
Fat	6.7g
Cholesterol	0.0mg
Sodium	24.5mg
Carbohydrates	14.2g
Protein	7.8g

* Percent Daily Values are based on a 2,000 calorie diet.

Old Bay Burgers

Ingredients

- 1 C. textured vegetable protein
- 1/4 C. quick-cooking rolled oats (not instant)
- 2 1/2 tsp Old Bay Seasoning
- 1/4 tsp ground black pepper
- 1/4 tsp mustard powder
- 3/4 C. water (almost boiling)
- 2 tbsps ketchup
- 2 tbsps soy sauce (or tamari or Bragg's)
- 1 tbsp tahini (or any other nut or seed butter)
- 2 tbsps nutritional yeast (flake kind, NOT powdered)
- 1/4 C. whole wheat pastry flour

Directions

- Get a mixing bowl: Add the oats, TVP, Old Bay, pepper and mustard. Mix them well. Add the water with soy sauce and ketchup. Whisk them well. Place the mix aside for 6 min.
- Stir in the tahini. Add the nutritional yeast and whole-wheat pastry flour. Mix them well. Shape the mix into 6 burgers.

- Place a large skillet on medium heat. Heat 2 1/2 tbsps of olive oil in it. Add the burgers and cook them for 8 min on each side. Assemble your burgers with your favorite toppings.
- Serve them right away.
- Enjoy.

Amount per serving: 6

Timing Information:

Preparation	15 mins
Total Time	30 mins

Nutritional Information:

Calories	57.4
Fat	1.7g
Cholesterol	0.0mg
Sodium	394.6mg
Carbohydrates	8.7g
Protein	2.8g

* Percent Daily Values are based on a 2,000 calorie diet.

Sesame Burgers

Ingredients

- 1 (15 ounce) cans cannellini, rinsed and drained
- 1/3 C. chopped onion (I use the frozen kind thawed out, this'd be one small onion)
- 2 garlic cloves, peeled
- 1 tbsp fresh parsley, chopped (or 1 tsp dried parsley)
- 2 tbsps nutritional yeast
- 2 tbsps sesame seeds (not tahini)
- 2 egg whites (or 1 whole egg)
- 1/2 C. breadcrumbs (I use whole-wheat)
- 1 tsp paprika
- 1/2 tsp sea salt
- 1/2 tsp black pepper
- 1 dash cayenne pepper

Directions

- Wash the beans with some fresh water. Place it in a colander to get remove the water.
- Get a food processor: Add the beans with rest of the ingredients. Pulse them several times until they become smooth. Transfer the mix into a bowl and cover it.

- Place it in the fridge for 45 min. Shape the mix into 4 burgers.
- Place a large skillet on medium heat. Heat the sesame oil in it. Add the burgers and cook them for 8 min on each side. Assemble your burgers with your favorite toppings.
- Serve them right away.
- Enjoy.

Amount per serving: 4

Timing Information:

Preparation	30 mins
Total Time	1 hr.

Nutritional Information:

Calories	186.4
Fat	3.0g
Cholesterol	0.0mg
Sodium	352.6mg
Carbohydrates	29.4g
Protein	11.9g

* Percent Daily Values are based on a 2,000 calorie diet.

Cajun Burgers with Lemon Sauce

Ingredients

- 1 (15 ounce) cans cannellini beans (drain liquid) or 1 (15 ounce) cans chickpeas (drain liquid)
- 1 egg
- 1 onion
- Approximately 1/2 C. breadcrumbs, crushed crackers or flour
- 1 tbsp minced garlic
- Salt and pepper
- 1 tbsp cumin (optional)
- Nonstick cooking spray

SEASONINGS (FEEL FREE TO MIX AND MATCH)

- Curry powder
- Garam masala
- Smoked paprika
- Minced chipotle pepper
- Cayenne
- Oregano
- Cajun seasoning
- Cheese

SAUCE

- 1/4 C. mayonnaise
- 2 -3 tbsps lemon juice
- 1 tbsp garlic powder or 1 tbsp minces garlic
- 1 chipotle pepper, minced (optional)

Directions

- Get a small bowl: Add the sauce ingredients. Whisk them well. Place the sauce in the fridge.
- Get a food processor: Add the garlic, onion bean and seasonings mix. Pulse them several times until they become finely chopped.
- Add the breadcrumbs with egg and flour. Mix them well. Shape the mix into 4 burgers.
- Place a large skillet on medium heat. Heat the sesame oil in it. Add the burgers and cook them for 8 min on each side. Assemble your burgers with the lemon sauce and your favorite toppings.
- Serve them right away.
- Enjoy.

Amount per serving: 4

Timing Information:

Preparation	10 mins
Total Time	15 mins

Nutritional Information:

Calories	246.9
Fat	6.5g
Cholesterol	56.6mg
Sodium	1130.1mg
Carbohydrates	35.9g
Protein	112.8g

* Percent Daily Values are based on a 2,000 calorie diet.

Oregon Inspired Burgers

Ingredients

BASE

- 4 C. water (divided into 2 C. each)
- 1 C. lentils (DO NOT SOAK AHEAD OF TIME!)
- 1 C. black rice
- 1/4 tsp salt
- 1 tbsp olive oil

FORMING STAGE

- 3/4 C. flour
- 1 tsp minced garlic (2 cloves, mashed and minced but I use the liquid stuff)
- 1 tsp kosher salt (or sea salt)
- 2 tsp tahini

DRY SEASONING

- 3/4 tsp paprika
- 1/2 tsp onion powder
- 1/4 tsp black pepper
- 1/4 tsp cayenne
- 1/4 tsp mustard (dry powdered mustard, not wet)
- 1 dash oregano

VEGGIES

- 1/4 C. peas
- 1/4 C. carrot
- 1/4 C. broccoli (I used the very fine chopped broccoli from the freezer section, florets are too big)
- 1/4 C. corn

THROW IN AT THE END

- 1/2 C. flour

Directions

- Before you do anything preheat the oven to 350 F. Grease a baking sheet.
- Cook the rice according to the directions on the package. Cook the lentils according to the directions on the package.
- Get a mixing bowl: Add the rice and lentils. Press them with a fork until they become slightly mashed. Add the garlic, kosher salt, and tahini. Mix them well.
- Stir in the flour gradually followed by the seasonings, veggies and the rest of the flour while mixing all the time. Place it aside for 12 min.
- Shape the mix into 12 burgers. Place them on the baking sheet. Cook them in the oven 16 min. Assemble your burgers with your favorite toppings. Serve them right away.
- Enjoy.

Amount per serving: 12

Timing Information:

Preparation	1 hr.
Total Time	1 hr. 15 mins

Nutritional Information:

Calories	149.8
Fat	1.9g
Cholesterol	0.0mg
Sodium	250.0mg
Carbohydrates	28.5g
Protein	4.4g

* Percent Daily Values are based on a 2,000 calorie diet.

Cereal Mayo Burgers

Ingredients

- 2 C. shredded carrots
- 2 eggs
- 1/2 C. mayonnaise
- 1 medium onion, minced
- 2 tbsps olive oil
- 1 clove garlic, chopped
- Salt and pepper to taste
- 6 C. soft bread crumbs
- 4 C. whole wheat flake cereal, crumbled

Directions

- Before you do anything preheat the oven to 375 F. Line up a baking sheet.
- Get a heatproof bowl: Add the carrot and microwave it for 4 min.
- Get a mixing bowl: Add the eggs, mayonnaise, onion, olive oil, garlic, salt, pepper, and carrots. Mix them well. Add the breadcrumbs and mix them again. Form the mix into 12 cakes.
- Place the cereal in a shallow pate. Coat the burgers with the cereal. Place the cakes in the baking sheet. Cook the

burgers in the oven for 14 min. Flip them and cook them for another 14 min.
- Assemble your burgers with your favorite toppings. Serve them right away.
- Enjoy.

Amount per serving 12

Timing Information:

Preparation	15 m
Cooking	25 m
Total Time	40 m

Nutritional Information:

Calories	206 kcal
Fat	11.5 g
Carbohydrates	122.5g
Protein	4.1 g
Cholesterol	34 mg
Sodium	300 mg

* Percent Daily Values are based on a 2,000 calorie diet.

Asian Italian Burgers with Cajun Mayo

Ingredients

- 4 large mushroom caps
- 1/2 C. soy sauce
- 1/2 C. Italian dressing
- 4 cloves garlic, chopped, or more to taste
- 1 large red bell pepper
- 1 C. reduced-fat mayonnaise
- 1 tbsp Cajun spice, or to taste
- 2 tbsp sriracha
- 4 hamburger buns split

Directions

- Get a zip lock bag: Add the mushroom with soy sauce, Italian dressing, and garlic. Shake the bag roughly to coat the ingredients. Place it aside for 2 h 30 min.
- Before you do anything heat the grill and grease it.
- Cook the bell pepper for 6 min on each side. Drain the mushroom caps from the marinade and cook them for 7 min on each side.

- Transfer the bell pepper to a zip lock bag and seal it and place them aside for 5 min sweat. Peel the bell peppers and chop them.
- Get a mixing bowl: Add the roasted bell pepper with mayo and Cajun spice. Mix them well. Place it in the fridge until ready to serve.
- Assemble your burgers with your favorite toppings then add an even amount of Sriracha to each. Serve them right away.
- Enjoy.

Amount per serving 4

Timing Information:

Preparation	15 m
Cooking	15 m
Total Time	2 h 40 m

Nutritional Information:

Calories	375 kcal
Fat	22.5 g
Carbohydrates	337.8g
Protein	7.1 g
Cholesterol	21 mg
Sodium	2459 mg

* Percent Daily Values are based on a 2,000 calorie diet.

London Shiitake Worcestershire Burgers

Ingredients

- 1 lb. fresh shiitake mushrooms, about 6 C. chopped finely
- 1 large onion, minced
- 2 slices white bread, finely diced
- 2 tbsps Worcestershire sauce
- 2 egg whites or 1 egg
- Salt
- Ground black pepper

Directions

- Place a large skillet on medium heat. Grease it with oil or cooking spray. Add the onion with mushroom and sauté them for 6 min. Add the bread dices with Worcestershire sauce. Sauté them for 1 min
- Turn off the heat. Place the mix aside to lose heat.
- Get a mixing bowl: Add the eggs and mix them well. Add the onion mix with salt and pepper. Mix them well. Shape the mix into 6 burgers.

- Place a large skillet on medium heat. Heat in it a splash of oil. Add the burgers and cook them for 8 min on each side.
- Assemble your burgers with your favorite toppings. Serve them right away.
- Enjoy.

Amount per serving: 6

Timing Information:

Preparation	20 mins
Total Time	30 mins

Nutritional Information:

Calories	54.5
Fat	0.5g
Cholesterol	0.0mg
Sodium	65.6mg
Carbohydrates	9.1g
Protein	4.4g

* Percent Daily Values are based on a 2,000 calorie diet.

Portobello Pepperjack Monterey Spicy Burgers

Ingredients

- 4 Portobello mushroom caps
- 1/4 C. balsamic vinegar
- 2 tbsps olive oil
- 1 tsp dried basil
- 1 tsp dried oregano
- 1 tbsp minced garlic
- Salt and pepper to taste
- 4 (1 ounce) slices Pepperjack cheese
- 4 slices Monterey cheese
- 1 tbsp diced jalapeno from a jar

Directions

- Before you do anything heat the grill and grease it.
- Get a mixing bowl: Add the vinegar, oil, basil, oregano, garlic, salt, and pepper. Mix them well to make the marinade.
- Stir the mushroom into the marinade. Place it aside for 18 min. Drain the mushroom and place the marinade aside.

- Cook the mushroom caps on the grill for 7 min on each side while basting them with the marinade every 2 min. Place the cheese slices on the mushroom while it is hot to melt.
- Assemble your burgers with your favorite toppings. Then evenly divide the diced jalapeno amongst the burgers.
- Enjoy.

Amount per serving 4

Timing Information:

Preparation	15 m
Cooking	20 m
Total Time	35 m

Nutritional Information:

Calories	203 kcal
Fat	14.6 g
Carbohydrates	9.8g
Protein	10.3 g
Cholesterol	20 mg
Sodium	259 mg

* Percent Daily Values are based on a 2,000 calorie diet.

Eggplant Patties with Cheddar

Ingredients

- 2 medium eggplants, peeled and cubed
- 1 C. shredded sharp Cheddar cheese
- 1 C. Italian seasoned bread crumbs
- 2 eggs, beaten
- 2 tbsps dried parsley
- 2 tbsps chopped onion
- 1 clove garlic, minced
- 1 C. vegetable oil for frying
- 1 tsp salt
- 1/2 tsp ground black pepper

Directions

- For 4 mins cook all the eggplants in the microwave on medium. Then flip the eggplants and cook for another 3 mins.
- Remove any resulting juices and mash the eggplants together.
- Add the following to the mashed eggplant: salt, cheese, garlic, bread crumbs, onions, parsley, and eggs.
- Now take your mix, and with your hands form as many patties as possible.

- For 6 mins per side cook the patties in hot oil.
- Enjoy on a bun, hamburger style.

Amount per serving (6 total)

Timing Information:

Preparation	Cooking	Total Time
15 m	20 m	35 m

Nutritional Information:

Calories	266 kcal
Fat	14.4 g
Carbohydrates	23.6g
Protein	12.4 g
Cholesterol	86 mg
Sodium	911 mg

* Percent Daily Values are based on a 2,000 calorie diet.

Horseradish Mushroom Burger I

Ingredients

- 2 Portobello mushroom caps
- 3 tsps horseradish sauce
- 2 leaves romaine lettuce
- 2 slices tomato
- 2 hamburger buns

Directions

- Cover a baking sheet with foil and then coat it with nonstick spray before setting your oven to 450 degrees before doing anything else.
- Cut the stem of your mushrooms off and then clean them under water.
- Now put the mushrooms on your baking sheet and cook them in the oven for 20 mins.
- Coat each of your buns with 1.5 tsps of horseradish and then a piece of tomato and lettuce on one bun. Top the other bun with a mushroom cap and form a burger.
- Enjoy.

Amount per serving (2 total)

Timing Information:

Preparation	Cooking	Total Time
5 m	15 m	20 m

Nutritional Information:

Calories	313 kcal
Fat	15.3 g
Carbohydrates	29.9g
Protein	15.5 g
Cholesterol	53 mg
Sodium	934 mg

* Percent Daily Values are based on a 2,000 calorie diet.

Zucchini Burgers

Ingredients

- 2 C. grated zucchini
- 2 eggs, beaten
- 1/4 C. diced onion
- 1/2 C. all-purpose flour
- 1/2 C. grated Parmesan cheese
- 1/2 C. shredded mozzarella cheese
- salt to taste
- 2 tbsps vegetable oil

Directions

- Get a bowl, combine: salt, zucchini, mozzarella, eggs, parmesan, flour, and onions.
- Combine the mix then get your oil hot.
- Once the veggie oil is hot, fry large dollops of the mix, until it is browned on both sides.
- Enjoy.

Amount per serving (4 total)

Timing Information:

Preparation	10 m
Cooking	20 m
Total Time	30 m

Nutritional Information:

Calories	245 kcal
Fat	14.7 g
Carbohydrates	15.7g
Protein	12.8 g
Cholesterol	111 mg
Sodium	282 mg

* Percent Daily Values are based on a 2,000 calorie diet.

THANKS FOR READING! JOIN THE CLUB AND KEEP ON COOKING WITH 6 MORE COOKBOOKS....

http://bit.ly/1TdrStv

To grab the box sets simply follow the link mentioned above, or tap one of book covers.

This will take you to a page where you can simply enter your email address and a PDF version of the box sets will be emailed to you.

Hope you are ready for some serious cooking!

http://bit.ly/1TdrStv

COME ON...
LET'S BE FRIENDS :)

We adore our readers and love connecting with them socially.

Like BookSumo on Facebook and let's get social!

Facebook

And also check out the BookSumo Cooking Blog.

Food Lover Blog

Printed in Great Britain
by Amazon